# The Big Outdoor Adventure

PHASE 5

7b

## Level 7 – Turquoise

# Helpful Hints for Reading at Home

The graphemes (written letters) and phonemes (units of sound) used throughout this series are aligned with Letters and Sounds. This offers a consistent approach to learning whether reading at home or in the classroom. Books levelled as 'a' are an introduction to this band. Readers can advance to 'b' where graphemes are consolidated and further graphemes are introduced.

**HERE IS A LIST OF ALTERNATIVE GRAPHEMES FOR THIS PHASE OF LEARNING. AN EXAMPLE OF THE PRONUNCIATION CAN BE FOUND IN BRACKETS.**

| Phase 5 Alternative Pronunciations of Graphemes | | | |
|---|---|---|---|
| a (hat, what) | e (bed, she) | i (fin, find) | o (hot, so) |
| u (but, unit) | c (cat, cent) | g (got, giant) | ow (cow, blow) |
| ie (tied, field) | ea (eat, bread) | er (farmer, herb) | ch (chin, school, chef) |
| y (yes, by, very) | ou (out, shoulder, could, you) | | |
| o_e (home) | u_e (rule) | | |

**HERE ARE SOME WORDS WHICH YOUR CHILD MAY FIND TRICKY.**

| Phase 5 Tricky Words | | | |
|---|---|---|---|
| oh | their | people | Mr |
| Mrs | looked | called | asked |
| could | | | |

**HERE ARE SOME WORDS THAT MIGHT NOT YET BE FULLY DECODABLE.**

| Challenge Words | | | |
|---|---|---|---|
| very | | | |

## TOP TIPS FOR HELPING YOUR CHILD TO READ:

• Allow children time to break down unfamiliar words into units of sound and then encourage children to string these sounds together to create the word.

• Encourage your child to point out any focus phonics when they are used.

• Read through the book more than once to grow confidence.

• Ask simple questions about the text to assess understanding.

• Encourage children to use illustrations as prompts.

PHASE 5

7b

This book is a 'b' level and is a turquoise level 7 book band.

# The Big Outdoor Adventure

**Written by**
Madeline Tyler

**Illustrated by**
Drue Rintoul

It was the school holidays and Rav was very, very bored. She had been stuck in the house for weeks!

Rav wanted to leave the house and explore, but Scout was too afraid. All noises made her jump and bounce like a little mouse.

"Come on, Scout," said Rav. "You can do it!
I can stay with you if you want me to."

But Scout was too afraid. She crouched down behind Rav's skirt, too afraid to look out of the window.

Rav pulled her skirt and twirled around. She wanted to go up mountains, jump in rivers and play in the dirt. Staying inside was boring!

"Just think of all the fun things we can do outside!" said Rav. "Don't you want to explore with me?"

Scout growled. She went to sneak underneath the chair, but not before Rav pounced on her.

"Too slow, Scout!" said Rav.

"Come on, Scout," said Rav. "We can go out together, you and me." Scout growled and crept to the door.

Rav took a picnic blanket out into the garden and laid it on the ground.
"I have treats out here!" called Rav.

Scout bounced out and looked around. There were tall mountains with lots of fir trees on. Some of the mountains were covered in snow.

Up high, there were lots of soft, white clouds that looked like bits of fluff.
"What can you see in the clouds, Scout?" asked Rav. "I can see bits of fluff."

Scout looked up and saw a mouse in a house, a big smiling mouth and a cowgirl riding a horse!

Cloud spotting was fun, but Rav wanted to explore some more. Rav found that resting for too long was very boring.

"Let's look for an adventure!" said Rav. She went back into the house and found all of her things for exploring.

"For our first adventure, let's look for a mountain to go up!" said Rav. "We can go all the way to the top!"

Scout felt nervous again. Cloud spotting was one thing, but climbing mountains was far more adventurous!

But Scout wanted to go. She wanted to go up mountains and walk in the fir tree forest. She told herself to be brave.

Scout was the first one outside and the first
one to reach the mountain.
"Wait for me, Scout!" shouted Rav.

Up they went. They reached where the snow fell and turned around.
"I can see our house from here!" said Rav.

As snow started to fall and block their house, they knew it was time to go back. But when they looked around they saw that they were lost.

They walked round and round, around the fir tree forest, but now they were even more lost than before!

Rav had a long, hard think.
"Let's go down," she said. So Rav and
Scout went south, back through the fir
tree forest.

Exhausted, they arrived home just as night started to fall. They were not lost! They were home!

"Let's stick to cloud spotting from now on!" said Rav. Scout nodded. It had been a long day, and they were pleased to be home.

Scout slouched down on the chair.
"I'm very proud of you, Scout," said Rav,
giving her a big hug.

Scout was no longer afraid, but she was worn out. Climbing mountains was hard work and now she was all set for a nap.

# The Big Outdoor Adventure

1. Why was Rav feeling bored?


2. Why do you think Scout might have been too afraid to go outside?


3. What did Rav see in the clouds?
   (a)   Bits of fluff
   (b)   A cowgirl on a horse
   (c)   An aeroplane


4. Where did Rav and Scout go on their adventure?


5. How do you think Rav and Scout were feeling while they were lost? Would you want to go on an adventure with Rav and Scout?

©2020 **BookLife Publishing Ltd.**
King's Lynn, Norfolk PE30 4LS

ISBN 978-1-83927-308-7

All rights reserved. Printed in Malaysia.
A catalogue record for this book is available
from the British Library.

**The Big Outdoor Adventure**
Written by Madeline Tyler
Illustrated by Drue Rintoul

# An Introduction to BookLife Readers...

Our Readers have been specifically created in line with the London Institute of Education's approach to book banding and are phonetically decodable and ordered to support each phase of the Letters and Sounds document.

Each book has been created to provide the best possible reading and learning experience. Our aim is to share our love of books with children, providing both emerging readers and prolific page-turners with beautiful books that are guaranteed to provoke interest and learning, regardless of ability.

**BOOK BAND GRADED** using the Institute of Education's approach to levelling.

**PHONETICALLY DECODABLE** supporting each phase of Letters and Sounds.

**EXERCISES AND QUESTIONS** to offer reinforcement and to ascertain comprehension.

**BEAUTIFULLY ILLUSTRATED** to inspire and provoke engagement, providing a variety of styles for the reader to enjoy whilst reading through the series.

AUTHOR INSIGHT:
**MADELINE TYLER**

Native to Norfolk, England, Madeline Tyler's intelligence and professionalism can be felt in the 50-plus books that she has written for BookLife Publishing. A graduate of Queen Mary University of London with a 1st Class degree in Comparative Literature, she also received a University Volunteering Award for helping children to read at a local school.

When she was a child, Madeline enjoyed playing the violin, and she now relaxes through yoga and reading books!

**PHASE 5**

**7b**

This book is a 'b' level and is a turquoise level 7 book band.